Permissible Pleasures

An Everyday Guide to the Abundant Life

MARGARET DARNELL

Copyright © 2020 Margaret Darnell
All rights reserved, including the right to reproduce this
book or portions thereof in any form whatsoever.

ISBN: 978-1-7356671-0-2

For Michael,
my hero,

and

"Rose Nose," "Bob," "Joy," and "Sman,"
our children

Table of Contents

Introduction 1

Part One:
The Pleasure of a Healthy Mindset (p. 4)

Our Thoughts Matter 5

Small Habits are Huge 7

Accepting Ourselves 8

Knowing Ourselves 10

Freedom From People-Pleasing 12

Not a Hot Mess Anymore 13

Serenity Prayer 15

Courage to Change 17

I wish I 18

Contentment and Gratitude 19

A Mattress Tag 24

To Compare or Not to Compare 27

Don't Ask "Why?"; Ask "What?" 28

Yesterday is History 30

Tomorrow is Your Future 31

Today is Your Life 33

Our Mark on the World 34

Part Two:
The Pleasure of Healthy Actions (p. 38)

Time for Some "Regenerizing" 38

Finding True Rest 39

A Big Pink Tub 40

Play First; Work Second 42

Busy-ness and Pleasure 43

Learning for the Fun of It 44

The Pleasure of Simple Joys 46

The Pleasure of an Unhurried Pace 49

The All Important Pleasure

of Rich Relationships 50

Date Night 55

Home, Sweet Home 57

Making Our Homes

Beautiful to the Eye 57

What About the Other Senses? 61

Clutter - The Homemaker's Arch Nemesis 64

An Unexpected Delight 66

A "Beckoning" Workspace 67

Exercise 67

Personal Clothing Style 71

Creating a Wardrobe We Love 72

Does Victoria Have a Secret? 75

A Note on Nighties and Fragrance 76

Hairstyle - Your Face's Best Accessory 77

Aging With Grace 78

Where Are the Spoons? How Routines Help 79

Might These Work for You? 81

Before New Year's Eve 82

Eat That Frog 83

The Bigger Pleasures 85

An Eating Plan for Life 86

A Little Caramel Cake 89

SF Agent 90

When Things Don't go as Planned 93

Some Musings on Cooking 93

Out of the Mouth of Babes 94

What are You Waiting For? 97

Coming Full Circle 98

Epilogue 100

Notes 103

Acknowledgements 109

Introduction

One day as my husband and I were leaving the gym after a hard workout, we stopped to converse briefly with the nice young man behind the front desk. As we openly rejoiced to the young man the relief that our workout was finished, and related our anticipation of a relaxing evening meal, he shared this quote with us:

"We will have to give account for every permissible pleasure that we forfeit."

~Rabbinical saying

The quote struck me; and stuck with me. It was somehow profoundly intriguing, and I couldn't get it out of my mind. After pondering it for a while I realized that it reminded me of my favorite Bible verse:

"Oh, taste and see that the Lord is good; how blessed is the man who takes refuge in Him!"

(~Psalm 34:8)

I've loved this verse for years, because it is more than just a verse. It is a **mindset**; a way of thinking. And I believe the quote about "permissible pleasures" captures that same mindset. As a Christian, I believe we are called to a

9

life of gratitude; a life of gratefulness for the love behind God's blessings, big and small.

We are designed in God's image, (Genesis 1:27) and we were designed to enjoy and appreciate all the permissible pleasures He affords us. Forfeiting them would be to brush Him off and take His love and blessings for granted. I believe instead, that He would have us bubbling over with zest for our God-given life, or as the French say, "joie de vivre," when we taste and see that He is good.

Part One

The Pleasure of a Healthy Mindset

One of the greatest gifts God gives us is the freedom to choose. He could have made us like the animals - preprogrammed by instinct. But He didn't. He gives us the permissible pleasure of choice.

Our choices lead to many of our feelings and experiences in life. They can determine the whole direction of our lives. The most important ones are to love God, pray, and serve others, and these are essential. But there are so many excellent books already written about these things, so that is not really what this book is about. Instead, I am writing about our mindset and some practical actions that will improve the quality of our daily lives. These are changes I have made in my own life, and they have made such a difference for me that I felt compelled to share them with others; to write it all down in a book. What, me? Write a book? Yes. In hopes that you read some idea or thought in it that truly changes your life for the better in some way. This is my constant prayer as I write, and it is my whole reason for making the effort to write this book.

Since what is on the inside of us is what will eventually show on the outside, I want to start by talking about our thought processes: our mental choices and attitudes affect everything else in our lives. This part (Part 1) is the hardest, but hopefully you will be very glad you stayed with me. Then we will get to all the joyful everyday permissible pleasures, too (Part 2).

~Our Thoughts Matter~

Our thought life is tremendously important, because it is a significant part of our inner person, or our "heart," as the Bible describes it. In fact, God tells us:

"Guard your heart above all things, *because out of it flow the springs of life.*" (~Prov. 4:23)

He is giving us the insight to recognize that our thoughts can affect how we feel (and how we act), and thus how we live our lives. Imagine the power our thoughts have over the quality and the direction of our lives. In recent years, behavioral scientists have confirmed what God's Word has already told us. They have "discovered" that our thoughts lead to our feelings and our actions, not the other way around.

Jesus said something about this, too. He said, "Out of the overflow of the heart, the mouth speaks. The good man brings good things out of the good stored up in him, and the evil man brings evil things out of the evil stored up in him." (~Matt. 12:34-35)

We think thousands of thoughts every day, so our mindset has the potential to greatly affect our spiritual, mental, emotional, and physical health. When the Bible talks about guarding our hearts, it is telling us to take responsibility for our thought life (our inner life). And the more we do this, the better our lives will be. There is only one person who can guard your heart and my heart. You and me. Nobody else can do it for us.

There is something else I have noticed...a healthy Christian is a Christian who makes a difference in this world. When we have a healthy mindset and thoughts, we will also have a very positive effect on those around us. Because when we are healthy, we are motivated by our love for God and other people rather than by our constantly changing emotions.

So how do we "guard our hearts"?

~Small Habits are Huge~

We do it one step at a time. Years ago, I did a Bible study called The Power of Small, by Jennifer Kennedy Dean. She sums the whole study up like this, "Every moment counts. Every decision matters. Every act has consequences. All big things start small... Our small decisions ultimately affect the outcome of major events." We should never underestimate the good that one tiny positive change can make in our lives over time. We just need to keep doing the next right thing, even if it is a tiny thing.

When our little "Rose Nose" was three years old, I decided to sew her a fancy dress. I hadn't sewn much before, so it took me a while. But I just did the next step on the pattern guide every time I got a chance. After a couple of months, I finally finished the dress. "Rose Nose" was so excited to wear it, and proudly told everyone, "My mama made this dress one seam at a time." A lot like our lives...one seam at a time. The results can be very beautiful.

I am writing this book to encourage you to think about possibilities. But to see them, you have to take an honest look at the way things are now, and how they have been in the past. I am not trying to make you feel guilty or "should" on yourself. If you do that, you are getting stuck. Please think past that. I want you to be encouraged as you read, thinking of all the possibilities in your future, as you pray for God's wisdom and take steps today to start in that direction.

Possibilities come from our freedom to choose, and this is a most generous gift from God. It is also exactly that: freedom. The exciting thing about it is that we can change course at any moment. If we haven't made the best choices up until now, He gives us the freedom to choose differently today.

~ Accepting Ourselves ~

We don't talk about this much, because it sounds prideful, but do you like yourself as a person? I don't mean it in a prideful way. Our thoughts about ourselves matter. Very much. Do you *like* the unique way the Lord put you together? Are you comfortable in your own skin, accepting who you are and how He made you? Do you like the personality He gave you? All the unique things and even the quirks that make you, you? I believe the Lord would like us to feel this way about ourselves.

Tim Keller says that humility is "not thinking less of yourself; it's thinking of yourself less." People who like and accept themselves are the most self-forgetful. They have settled the issues of self-consciousness and inadequacy, and are free to have an outward focus. It is hard to be truly others-centered when you have a deep seated fear of inadequacy gnawing at you from the inside.

How do you picture yourself? More importantly, how do you talk to yourself? I heard a story on You-Tube about a girl whose husband had left her. She was devastated for a long time, but eventually decided to start dating again. There was a man who had shown a lot of interest in her online and asked her out for dinner, so she agreed to meet him. After they conversed for a few minutes at the restaurant, she realized he wasn't having a good time. He ended their date early. She called her best friend and told her the situation. Her best friend said, "Well, what do you expect? You have big hips; you have nothing interesting to say. Why would a handsome, successful man like that ever go out with a loser like you?" Actually, the You-Tube speaker said, she didn't call her best friend. This is what she told herself.

That story hit me right between the eyes. I started paying attention to the things I was telling myself. To be honest, I wasn't guarding my heart very well. What kinds of things do you tell yourself on a regular basis?

For example, if you catch a glance of yourself in the mirror when you are getting dressed, what thoughts pass through your mind? Sometimes we say things to ourselves that we would *never* say to our friends. We need to talk to ourselves with the same kindness and compassion that we'd give our best friend. When we start telling ourselves negative things, we need to picture our best friend's face. How would we respond to her in the very same situation? What tone of voice would we use? What words and facial expressions? What would we say to encourage her and help her try again?

For years, I have teased my friends when they say something less than flattering about themselves, "Don't talk about my friend that way." Occasionally, I need to take my own advice. We all need to pay attention to what we tell ourselves. Because over time, even the smallest thoughts we repeat to ourselves become "facts" in our own minds.

~Knowing Ourselves~

God wants us to know who we are; to be self-aware. The encouraging part of self-awareness is recognizing the remarkable things about ourselves as individuals. It is healthy to know our God-given strengths and talents, and to respect our unique gifts. It's also healthy to ask for His help in working to develop them. Eventually we will have the joy of using them to encourage and bless others. There is incredible fulfillment in this.

The other part of self-awareness is seeing the "shadow side" of ourselves and our personalities. How well do we really know ourselves? Do we see our negative tendencies, and those things in us that are not OK and need God's forgiveness? And many times we have unhealthy thought patterns we aren't even aware of; each different personality type has tendencies to think in certain (not-so-great) ways. Sometimes patterns we learned from our family during childhood are so automatic, we don't even realize they are affecting us. And bad experiences we have had in life often affect our thoughts about ourselves below the surface.

Understanding the good, the bad, and the ugly about ourselves is tough. But when we are gut-level honest about it is when we experience real freedom. Because when we see our own faults and sins for what they really are, we are also very honest with God. And we really mean it when we ask Him to forgive us. We see our own gaping need. And it never ceases to amaze me that He actually *wants* to forgive us. Even if we have to ask Him a thousand times a day. He always forgives us when we ask. But sometimes, after we have asked God for forgiveness, we have a hard time forgiving ourselves.

We are our own problem. We refuse to show ourselves the mercy that God has already shown us. So if God has forgiven you, what is keeping you from forgiving yourself?

~Freedom From People-Pleasing~

Knowing who we are (and liking who we are) saves us from a whole lot of unnecessary trouble. We won't waste time worrying about others' opinions of us, because liking and accepting ourselves does not depend on other people's opinions of us. We don't wonder "What will they think about me?" We have freedom from what "they" think. Who is the "they" in your life, and do they really even exist? We won't make a habit of replaying conversations in our heads wondering what others thought of our comments. We can say no when we need to, because we are not worried about someone disliking us if we do that. We don't need others to make us feel good about ourselves, because we already like and feel good about ourselves. We won't have what the Bible calls "fear of man." People pleasing. A concern and love for others, yes; a fear of what they think of us, no. This is great freedom: knowing that if we have pleased God, all is well. What a gratifying way to live.

~ Not a Hot Mess Anymore ~

Have you ever felt like you are broken or a perpetual hot mess? I've got some good news for you. When Christ comes into your life, you are no longer broken. Read that again, please. No longer broken. Yes, there may be things that need to change in your life, but you are now a "good work in progress." He tells us that the old things in our lives are gone, and we are a new creation.

It kind of reminds me of when my husband and I were part of the Iron Tribe Fitness program. Iron Tribe is a CrossFit type program, or as my husband says, "CrossFit without the crazy." Everyone who participated was called an "Iron Tribe Athlete." It didn't matter whether you were twenty or seventy years old, how much weight you could lift, or if you could keep up with the routine. Once you signed up as a member, you were referred to as an athlete, even on your first day at the gym. You might not feel like an athlete, but you were considered one. And all the athletes were a work in progress.

Our pastor often says, "God loves you just the way you are, but He loves you too much to let you stay that way." When Christ gets hold of our lives, the Holy Spirit often will begin to change us in specific ways. On some days we can see our forward progress; on other days, not so much. But just because we can't see it doesn't mean it's not there. We have to be patient. We don't expect a two year old to be able to do what a twenty-six year old can do. In the same way, God knows exactly where we are in our spiritual development. He works with each of us individually according to where we are to make us pure; to make us more like Jesus. And even when it's uncomfortable, it is exciting to know we are on our way to realizing our full potential; we're like a flower coming into full bloom.

We will have our challenges and disappointments (and failures, too - which are painful). But that is part of growing and being on our way to *better*. As a kid, I remember my grandmama asking me, "Are you having growing pains, honey?" That's because growing is uncomfortable; but sometimes "life begins at the end of our comfort zone."

So the next time you have some "growing pains," please remember to look back afterwards and rejoice in all the things you have learned and how far you've come. Because God never wastes our tears or struggles. He is too kind to do that. You will come out better than before.

I love what Charles Stanley says: "Anything that God does in your life will last. It will be for your perfection, your wholeness. And it will endure throughout all the ages. What Christ is doing in you day by day...is a good work that has eternal value. You are not only a work in progress, but you are a *good* work in progress."

~Serenity Prayer~

You are probably familiar with the Serenity Prayer; in fact, you may even have a coffee cup or cross-stitch of it somewhere in your house:

"God, grant me the serenity to accept the things I cannot change; courage to change the things I can; and wisdom to know the difference."

When I read it, I think of three things. First, I should always ask God for wisdom. Second, there are some things that are "above my pay grade" and are none of my business (that would be the part about accepting the things I cannot change). And third - "I say this with all the love that I can" (as our preacher used to say before telling us something we might not want to hear) - I need to get off my duff and do the part that is my business. Have the courage to change the things I can. There is God's part, and there is our part, and keeping those straight is essential to having peace of mind.

God's part is the things in life we can't change; the things we have no control over. We quickly lose our peace of mind when we try to take over God's part. It is best to pray and leave those things in His hands. This is where ideas like "Bloom where you're planted" and "God's got this" are great advice. What happens when we try to take responsibility for God's part? Well, for one thing, we waste our "fighting" energy that could be spent changing the things we actually can change.

And we also become absolutely miserable. We try to control things, situations, and people. This does not work. And because we can't control them, we become angry, or cause others to become angry. We grow depressed, or deeply worried, living in fear and chronic anxiety about what might happen. That's because we were never intended to carry that load. That is God's part.

But then there is our part. These are the actions we can take to make our situation better. The things we do have control over. This is where ideas like "Bloom where you're planted" and "God's got this" are not great advice at all. They are excuses that keep us from being courageous and doing what we need to do. If we are not trying to improve our situation, we are probably making excuses, and that never leads to peace of mind. In fact, it will destroy it.

Like I told you in the beginning, I am not saying this to make you feel guilty. I just want us to be honest with ourselves and think about it. There are so many things we have the ability to change that can make an amazing difference in our lives. But we have to know what they are before we can do them.

It is so easy to think, "Well, what can you do?" This leads to being passive and resigned, and to having blind spots. I often ask the Lord if there is any situation, relationship, or area in my life that can be better...even a little bit. Is there something I can do, whether it is making a major change or a simple one?

~Courage to Change~

It is human nature to love the familiar. Not making change often feels good, because it is more comfortable; like a favorite pair of leather shoes that has softened and conformed to our feet. There is a feeling of security in clinging to what we know. Making change is uncomfortable - especially at first - and that is why we don't like to do it. But it is normal to feel that way. Maya Angelou understood this when she said, "We delight in the beauty of the butterfly, but rarely admit the changes it has gone through to achieve that beauty."

That is why we have to pray for "the courage to change the things we can." People who have courage are not necessarily braver than the rest of us. Having courage means to "do it afraid": to step out and do things in spite of how we feel. If we can accept the fact that change is uncomfortable and learn to keep going anyway, we will have a life worth living. We will have richer relationships, broader experiences, and develop our gifts. Simply put, when we are courageous, we will live life to the full.

~ I wish I... ~

For example, how would you finish this sentence? "I wish I..." When you consider your wishes, which ones are things that you simply can't change, and which ones could you possibly change? Ask God for wisdom to know the difference, because today is the day you can begin making one of those wishes come true. Let me give you an everyday example. Say you wish you could lose that last 15 pounds. If you walk 20 minutes a day, by the end of this year you will be lighter and more in shape than you are today, even if you don't change a single thing in your diet. Or you could cut just a hundred calories a day from your current diet; that's pretty easy to do. But over time, this simple change will yield results.

Sometimes we feel like we have to change everything overnight, but we don't. That kind of thinking paralyzes and overwhelms us. Then we feel helpless and don't do anything. You are not helpless. You can do something. Fiona Ferris says, "Don't discount any action as being 'too small,' for it could be there where real transformation takes place, seemingly without effort. Choose one thing and start today."

~Contentment and Gratitude~

Silvia was beautiful and radiant. This small Guatemalan woman had just cooked a large meal for our missionary team using a fire in the floor of a concession hut. She and her friends kept our food warm by floating bowls of food in a (clean) trash barrel filled with hot water. After we had all enjoyed our meal, we were sitting under a tree talking. I asked her through our interpreter, "What gives you such joy?" She said, "Every day is a gift, and God is so good to me. He gives me everything that I need." Her smile could melt the Abominable Snowman, and the light in her eyes was genuine.

This woman lived in a dirt-floored house with no windows. No indoor plumbing. Probably two pairs of shoes. Yet her joy bubbled out of her and was unstoppable. It came from her way of thinking; her mindset. She trusted the goodness of God, and saw everything through that filter. She appreciated the blessings that she had, and she was content. I could see from Silvia's example that even though circumstances certainly affect us, they don't necessarily determine the quality of our lives.

There was also in that little Guatemalan village a woman who appeared to have more money than the rest of the villagers. She wore bright clothes and jewelry, something the other villagers didn't have. She knew she was the town "hottie," and yet of all the people we met in that village, she seemed the most unsettled and miserable. Having more money and being more beautiful than the others did not mean she had a better life.

Dale Carnegie famously said, "It isn't what you have or who you are or where you are or what you are doing that makes you happy or unhappy. It is what you think about."

And the apostle Paul steers us towards contentment and gratitude when he wrote:

"Rejoice always. Pray without ceasing. *Give thanks in everything*, for this is God's will for you in Christ Jesus."
~1 Thessalonians 5:16-17

and

"...But godliness with contentment is great gain."
~ 1 Tim. 6:6

Our lives are the richest when we are grateful and content. I saw a Facebook quote that said, "Talking about our problems is our greatest addiction. Break the habit and talk about your joys." That's pretty good advice. But to talk about our joys, we have to - you guessed it - think about them. So let me ask you, what do you love about your life right now? Have you ever tried to list all the blessings God has given you?

Ann Voskamp did, and she tells about it in her book <u>One Thousand Gifts</u>. When she was terribly discouraged, she wrote down one thousand things she was thankful for. As you can imagine, it took her a while; but it changed her life, because it changed her mindset. After I read her book, I bought myself a pretty little notebook, and now each morning, I write down three things in it that I'm grateful for. The catch is, I can't repeat. That means I am always looking for and paying attention to new blessings. But it also made me realize how many repeated blessings I have in my life that I used to take for granted. I would highly recommend starting a gratitude journal. But if you don't like to actually write things down, you might try to think of three things before you go to bed at night or in the morning over your cup of coffee.

If you haven't done this before, you might not know where to start, so here are a few thoughts to get you rolling. I consider things like a hot meal, a hot shower, and a roof over our heads to be great gifts to us. Think about what people used to have to do to enjoy a hot meal. They had to chop down a tree or gather wood to build a fire. Imagine having to do that every single time you wanted your food heated. That is a lot of labor. Today, we can turn a knob or push a microwave button and quickly heat our meal. And how about the fact that we don't have to catch our food or find some plant or berry to eat every time we're hungry? I find that amazing. How very, very blessed we are.

A hot shower is also a tremendous gift to us. In centuries past, only the very privileged few even had the luxury of a private hot bath, and it was an occasional event, not a daily one. It required someone having to heat many buckets of water over a fire and pour them into a tub one by one. You can see why this wasn't a daily luxury. Now, not only can we have a daily hot bath if we would like, but we can also have the water sprayed down over us continuously until we are finished bathing. Not freezing cold water, but soothing warm water. Anytime we feel like it - and in private, too. Isn't that an amazing privilege when you stop to think about it?

How about a good roof over our heads? Did you have to build the house you are living in with your own hands? Chances are good that you didn't, yet most of us live in a home that is safe and clean; no dirt floors and fleas and rats. Glass windows that keep out the bugs and the heat and the freezing cold air. And, of course, indoor heating and cooling, so we can stay comfortable. Locks on the doors to keep us safe. And then there is a constant supply of fresh water, indoor plumbing instead of outhouses, and electricity that supplies our many appliances and conveniences. (For a minute, imagine how life would be without your refrigerator and freezer.) And if that weren't enough already, we have beautifully painted or wallpapered walls and coordinated decor. We live better than anybody in history ever has before.

How about this one? If you wear corrective lenses, think about centuries ago when someone with poor eyesight just had to stumble through life. There was no help for them. I wear glasses myself, and have gone from complaining about having to wear them to incredible gratitude that they are even available to me.

I think you get the idea. But those are just physical blessings. How about the intangible blessings? Fred

Rogers, of *Mr. Roger's Neighborhood* fame, once gave a graduation speech that became known as his "one minute of silence" speech. In the talk, he asked everyone to sit quietly for one minute and think about the people in their lives who had loved and encouraged them. People who wanted the best for them and helped them become who they are today. I am sure there are people in your life like that; I've certainly had some in mine, too. If they are still alive, today is a great time for us to let them know what a tremendous impact they have had on us. There is nothing like putting gratitude into action.

Another tip that has helped me feel more grateful is spending at least twenty seconds thinking about something I am grateful for before moving on to other thoughts. It sounds like a short amount of time, but you would be surprised. Try it and see.

~A Mattress Tag~

When our son "Sman" was small, we affectionately called him a "party in a box." He could make fun out of absolutely nothing. His siblings joked, "Just hand 'Sman' a mattress tag, and he'll be happy." He did not forfeit *any* permissible pleasures. There's a lot to be said for taking great joy in small pleasures. What are some of the small pleasures (mattress tags) of your everyday life? In At Home with Madame Chic, Jennifer Scott talks about the "pleasures of the morning, the afternoon, and the evening." I like that idea. One of the pleasures of the morning for me is enjoying my large mug of coffee and a simple and hearty breakfast on the back porch before I start work. Do you have a favorite morning pleasure? Morning pleasures might include hugging your loved ones, listening to your favorite morning broadcast or reading the paper. Maybe you take your pet out in the early morning and enjoy the sunrise.

I like to have a "quiet time" in the morning; read my Bible and pray... to be still before God, like Psalm 46:10 says. Doing this first every day feels like starting to water ski with the ski rope in my hands, rather than wrapped around my ankles. I also enjoy a hot shower and getting dressed in an outfit I love. Putting on a little makeup and jewelry and fragrance. It feels so good to face the day with confidence and poise.

The afternoon has its pleasures, too. If you have small children, their afternoon naptime might be the only chance for you to put up your feet and gather your own thoughts. Since I work from home, afternoons are often when I run errands. It is a welcome change of pace to deliver our product shipments to FedEx or go to the bank; I look forward to chatting with the people I see on my regular errands. If I plan to assemble products or work at my desk rather than run errands, I will usually take a fifteen minute break in the middle of the afternoon to get a cup of tea (or an iced drink if it's hot outside) and read on the back porch. Then, when I get back to work, I feel very refreshed.

If you are not employed, some afternoon pleasures might include things like working on a hobby, cooking, gardening, shopping, getting your nails done, or meeting with a friend.

And then there are the pleasures of the evening. The crickets are starting to sing outside, and dusk is settling in. Most of us are usually in the kitchen cooking something delicious for dinner at this point. There is the pleasure of the meal itself, and once everything is tidied back up (and the kids are tucked in bed), there is some time to totally unwind. Ahhh. Time to enjoy the pleasure of putting our feet up and lounging after a full day.

And last, but definitely not least, time alone with our spouse can be quite a great pleasure of the morning, afternoon, *or* evening. Wink.

~To Compare or Not to Compare~

We live in a world of comparisons. We compare prices and options; we compare the gas mileage of cars we consider buying - or compare horsepower, like my husband does. Comparisons can help us make excellent choices.

The trouble comes when we compare our life to someone else's life. There is no way to compare apples to apples when we compare ourselves with others. In the end, we are comparing our inside to their outside. And there is no way that will ever be a fair comparison ... or an accurate one.

There is no problem in letting someone inspire us in a particular area. This is what mentoring is all about. But we need to eradicate the mental habit of comparing ourselves with others, because it can make us feel either inferior or superior, both of which are very destructive. Comparing can be at the root of two of the worst sins: coveting and pride. Feelings of inferiority sometimes lead to coveting, and feelings of superiority can lead to pride. These sins can wreck our lives. No good can come from comparing ourselves with others.

Instead, I believe the Lord would have us compare ourselves with ourselves. For example, who are we today compared to who we were five, ten, or fifteen years ago? This kind of comparison is constructive and helps us live an examined life. Because if we aren't pleased with the comparison of our past with our present, we can begin to change that today. We can get out of our rut and avoid regrets. But if we have made great progress in our life, we can see how far we have come, and that is both encouraging and also great motivation to continue.

~Don't Ask "Why?"; Ask "What?"~

I have noticed that when a problem comes along in my life, how I frame the situation in my thoughts makes all the difference. Asking "Why?" is not constructive. If I ask why, then it is easy to start complaining. Or blaming. Or feeling like a victim. And (I say this with all the love that I can) it can occasionally come from having an entitlement mindset. We did not get or do not have what we think we should: what we feel entitled to. It would be wise to examine why we think we are owed these things in the first place. Feeling entitled can be very destructive to us, and will not help us have a healthy response to difficulties in life.

It helps me more to ask "What?". Maybe "What is the solution?" or "What is the next step?". Sometimes there might not be anything I can do about the situation. Then "What can I learn from this?" or "What can I do to make this easier?" are constructive questions. This keeps me looking forward.

I also want to look upward. I love what Nahum 1:7 says, "The Lord is good, a refuge in times of trouble. He cares for those who trust in Him..." It is healthy to accept that life is going to have both good and bad times. Maybe even a few terrible times. This is just a part of the human experience. Every person will experience these things at some time or another.

But even during challenges, we can experience that He is good, and that He listens and notices what we are going through. He has compassion towards us and never leaves us to walk alone. He hears and answers us. He may not always answer the exact way we are expecting, but He will be kind in the way that He does answer. Someone once asked Tim Keller if God answers all our prayers, and he responded, "God will either give us what we ask for in prayer, or He will give us what we would've asked for if we knew everything He knows."

~Yesterday is History~

One night my husband Michael was talking about the movie, *The Gumball Rally*, and he was surprised that I had never seen it, so we watched it. One of my favorite parts was the scene where the Italian race car driver was explaining to the other driver the rules of racing. He explains the first rule as he rips the rearview mirror off the windshield and says in his thick Italian accent, "Whats-a behind me is-a not important."

A few years ago we saw a show where a woman was bemoaning the "No Regerts" tattoo that covered the length of her thigh. Michael jokingly said that if he ever opened a tattoo removal business, he would name it "No Regerts". We all have things we wish we had done differently in our past; we all have our "regerts." This is also a part of being human. Thankfully, God has a way of redeeming our regrets.

It is wise to learn from our past. Our past is only a failure if we don't learn from it. So "whats-a behind me" is important. But it does not define who we are. It does not create our future. And it does not determine what we get to think and do today.

~Tomorrow is Your Future~

"You can't go back and change the beginning, but you can start where you are and change the ending."

~ C.S. Lewis

Sometimes, I think we have a love-hate relationship with the future. Our imaginations are so powerful, that when we picture something in our minds, we experience all the emotions as if that future scenario is true. And since we're bringing the emotion of that imagined future into today, we need to be *very* selective about what we tell ourselves... what type of future that we allow ourselves to picture in our minds.

When I feel worried, afraid, or overwhelmed, I am usually imagining some negative picture of the future. Humans naturally tend to do this. Our brain has a greater sensitivity to bad news than to good. Scientists call this the "negativity bias," and it is tied in with our survival instinct. In an emergency, this tendency can serve us well, but it can be terrible for our health if it is our way of thinking everyday. Our bodies react to an imaginary bad situation by releasing stress hormones just as if the situation were real. And our emotions react, too: picturing a negative future situation makes us forget that at this exact present moment, we are OK. Because even if we are OK, we surely don't feel like it. We feel the unnecessary pain of future troubles that don't yet exist and may never exist.

But what if we used our imaginations to dwell on all the possibilities instead? If we can feel all the bad emotions of imagining a negative future, then couldn't we also feel the exciting emotions of imagining a positive future?

For example, what if we pray about a troubling situation and then picture the point in time where God has already answered us? How would we feel at that point? Or we can imagine the things we would like to do or create. Lena Kay says: "Everything on this planet, besides what God has created, was once an idea in the mind of a human being." And also, she continues, we should picture ourselves five years from now, and how each area in our lives is great. Would we feel different? Yes. Well, (by imagining it) we can feel that way now and begin to take steps towards the "me of five years from now."

Coach Justin at Iron Tribe Fitness posted this: "Your mind must reach the destination before your body does." Of course, he was talking about physical fitness - getting in shape - but this is true in every area of life.

Picturing who we would like to become in the future helps us determine the steps we need to take to get there.

We begin to live and think and act like that person we want to become; to think of ourselves as that person. Brian Tracy says that our mental picture of ourselves has a powerful effect on our behavior, and how we view ourselves on the inside largely determines our performance on the outside.

And here is another thought. We can do the same thing for the other people in our lives. We can treat them as the person they are becoming, not who they are today. We are never too old to start doing this, and it is never too late...

~Today is Your Life~

Live *today*. This is the gift God has given you. The past is behind you. The future is not yours yet.

Writing this part is a little difficult for me. Two weeks before Christmas this year, my Mama received a terminal bone cancer diagnosis. A terminal diagnosis makes you start asking some big questions. I remember asking Mama, "What are some things you would like to do before you die?" She smiled and said, "You know, I've always wanted to try my hand at art." Glad that there was something I could do for her, I immediately bought her some paint, art supplies, and adult coloring books - and she enjoyed them very much.

I prayed that she would live well until the end and not suffer. I talked with her the day before she died. She was low on energy, but she was busy planning a get-together at her house for her local Arts Club. She and a friend planned to entertain her guests by playing piano duets. The day after I talked with her, she fell and within twenty-four hours she was gone.

Her passing has reminded me to live each day with intention. To be mindful of the present moment and slow down. To try to make things better, not perfect. To linger a little bit. Also, I don't want to wait to think about the things I'd love to do "one day." Today is "one day." I have asked myself this question, and I am asking you, too. Is there something you've always wanted to do, but never have? Now is the time.

~Our Mark on the World~

An old high school friend posted this on Facebook a while back: "If you do one kind thing for someone every day, at the end of the year, you will have done 365 kind things." It's encouraging how small and steady adds up. That's the kind of math I can do.

I think we all want our lives to make a difference in this world. Often, we look for that big purpose of our lives, not realizing that the small things we do each day might be the most important things. Ann Voskamp says, "Do we ever really know which mark we make matters the most?" Only God knows which little kindness we've done will make the biggest eternal difference. One day we may be very surprised to learn that some small thing we've long since forgotten was the seed that eventually became a great harvest. So when you hear His still, small voice prompting you to do a little something for someone, do it. Right then. You never know.

Sometimes it is easy not to realize the value of what we do, because we are just "doing daily life". We may feel unnoticed and unimportant. But this is just a feeling, not a fact. (And we might want to examine what we're telling ourselves that leads us to that feeling.) Picturing Jesus standing right there in front of me helps me do everything like I'm doing it for Him... and He notices. One day we will understand just how much He notices.

I once read a story about a missionary who was returning home on an ocean liner from years in the mission field. Also on that ship was a well-known politician who was returning from a foreign relations trip. When the boat docked in the harbor, there was a ticker tape parade and elaborate celebration welcoming the politician back home into the country, but the missionary silently left the ship unnoticed. He prayed, "Lord, I feel so unimportant. I've spent all these years serving you in a foreign country, and now nobody even knows I'm here." The Lord answered him, "That's because you're not home yet."

Part Two

The Pleasure of Healthy Actions

~Time for Some "Regenerizing"~

I love this word my friend Yvette accidentally made up: "regenerizing." We laughed about it the first time she said it, and we have used it ever since. It really is a great word. I think she was trying to say "re-energize", but it came out as this crazy combination of "regenerate" and "energize." And I believe "regenerizing" is one of God's permissible pleasures for us.

A few years ago, I got to visit Israel. In Jerusalem, our meals were catered by our hotel. There were lavish buffets with many meats, fresh vegetables, fruits, breads, and desserts, and I was quickly getting spoiled. So I was totally surprised by our breakfast on the Sabbath: A small number of workers set out some leftovers for us, and some instant coffee was available. That is it. They just didn't work on the Sabbath, and it made such an impression on me.

45

I began to think about my own life and the Ten Commandments. As a Christian, I still live by those commandments. Except maybe I had missed one. Remembering the Sabbath and keeping it holy. Working six days, but resting on the seventh, just like our Father did when He created everything. Jesus even told his followers that we weren't made for the Sabbath; it was made for us. How had I missed that?

In our defense, our culture applauds hard work and diligence, and so does God. But God also knows we need a break sometimes. And the commandment about the Sabbath is just that...His telling us to slow down; giving us permission to rest and refresh ourselves. Taking time to think about Him and the things that matter most.

My Sundays look a lot different now. And when I wake up on Sunday morning, I get that same feeling of anticipation like I did as a kid when I realized it was Christmas morning.

~ Finding True Rest ~

When King David said in the Psalms, "I am at rest in God alone," (Psalm 62:1) I think he was talking about something we can all relate to: the human desire for rest, peace of mind, and a sense of place. We long for this regardless of what season of life we are in. And I believe this longing is filled by spending time with the One who made us. He can speak to us in ways deeper than any human can. The most important part of the Sabbath for me is making the time to talk with Him and read His words. And I can relate to King David... when I spend time with God is when I am truly at rest.

~ A Big Pink Tub ~

I love my home. I really do. But it was built in the 1990's when mauve, teal, and black were all the rage. So were bright brassy fixtures; and all of that was topped off with flame stitch patterns. Don't worry - we have been steadily repainting and updating since we moved here. The main reason we couldn't resist this house is the pretty lake behind us and the screened-in porch overlooking it.

From my back porch, I have learned a lot about otters, snakes, turtles, beavers, and herons. Ducks and geese, too. It surprises me that the rabbits and squirrels now recognize the sound of my voice and don't run away. They just carry on with their activities, ignoring me like I am a tree or a rock. Our house is right smack dab in the middle of town, but somehow the animals didn't get the memo. They know a good water source when they see one. (I think there is a sermon in there somewhere.)

Oh, and did I mention the big pink Jacuzzi tub? Yes, pink. While we have gotten most of the rest of the house looking like an upscale lake cabin, we had left that bathroom as a project for later, knowing that it might be an ambitious undertaking and probably expensive, too. Finally, during the COVID quarantine, we decided to make some small improvements to see if it would make a difference. My husband, Michael, thought we might just be "putting lipstick on a pig," but we were both hopeful. It is amazing what fresh paint, new light fixtures, and fancy faucets can do for a room. We painted the wall behind the tub a rich red and hung a draped sheer curtain; added some plants and candles, and a spa stand in the corner, filled with enticing bath salts and goodies. I never thought I'd say this, but I love that pink tub now.

What does that pink tub have to do with Sundays? Well, a lot. It is one of my permissible pleasures each week. I truly look forward to my bath with handfuls of delicious smelling bath salts. My favorite scented candles lit. Beautiful music playing on the stereo. But wait, there's more. What bath wouldn't be complete without some special delicacies served on a crystal plate and a treat drink to accompany it? And to top it all off, some intriguing book (or audio book) to read while I luxuriate?

And time. Just time to slow down and relax. It's amazing how these simple pleasures make me feel like I'm on vacation at a five star hotel... and it is absolutely "regenerizing."

~Play First; Work Second~

"Play first; work second. It stimulates our passion." Dr. Shimi Kang says. This can be another way of honoring the Sabbath. It can be "playing first." What things are play for you? When is the last time you have done them? Imagine if you spent a whole day each week doing them. It is heavenly. For me, time with Michael is play, and so is playing the piano or guitar. Or I might spend an afternoon reading on the porch; try some art project; bake a delicious treat; or attend a car show with Michael. It's great to sit in lawn chairs under a tent (thank you, Chuck and Lynn) at a car show and catch up with our friends. It reminds me of the days when people gathered on their front porches to visit. And there's nothing like cruisin' down a winding country road with the T-tops out in our '84 TransAm. Definitely regenerizing.

~Busy-ness and Pleasure~

Busy-ness seems like a badge of honor in our culture. I used to feel a little guilty if I wasn't doing something productive, but I don't anymore. Now I know better: resting is productive, too. Think of the renewed energy you have after you have had a good break.

But with so much on our plates, it is really hard to get any rest in the middle of a busy week. Years ago, Andy Stanley talked about an idea called time margin. He compared it to the white area of space around the words on the pages of a book. Picture this in your mind for a minute: imagine that the words filled each page from edge to edge. From the top to bottom edge; from side to side. Your eye would have no idea where to focus!

That is how our lives are, too, if we don't have any time margin. If we stay booked solid, rushing from one activity to another without a little down time in between, we will lose our focus.... and burn out. Down time gives us the mental break we need to stay energized, and it renews our joy and contentment.

Have you ever noticed that sometimes your most inspired ideas come to you in the shower? Your best ideas that could possibly change your life or others' lives in some way? That is because most of us have a few moments of time margin when we are in the shower. (My husband says "the toilet," but we won't go there.) A little mental space. It is in that space that we will often have our most creative ideas and thoughts.

The secret is to give yourself a few minutes specifically to stop and enjoy a small pleasure at various times throughout your day. To have a little "time margin" automatically built-in to your daily routine. Make sure that these pleasures are something you really look forward to. This will help you anticipate your work breaks and feel that you are really living...not just working all the time. You may be working hard, but you are still taking time to smell the roses.

~ Learning for the Fun of It ~

During a phone conversation the other night, our son "Bob" made the comment, "You can't outsource insight." I thought that was profound. And God has promised to give us wisdom and insight if we will ask. Wisdom and insight are priceless.

But God has also given us another generous gift: our ability to learn. I don't want to admit this, but every time I pass the high school near our house, I think to myself, "I'm so glad I'm finished with school and never have to go back!" I do not miss the tests, the pressure of exams and speeches, and term papers. After finally finishing my Masters degree, I have not *even* looked back.

But that doesn't mean I have quit learning. Not at all. It means that learning has *just gotten a whole lot more fun.* I get to pick books I want to read. If I write, the teacher doesn't pick the topic. Now I get to learn history by watching movies and interesting documentaries, and the details stick with me so much better that way. I am learning about all kinds of things that weren't even available to me back when I was in school.

We live in such an unprecedented time in human history. The resources available to us are unbelievable and at our fingertips. All kinds of digital media. How-to videos, podcasts, blogs, and even Bible apps. I don't think we can dream up a topic that we can't find somewhere on the "Interwebs." If you want to learn a new skill or see how to fix something, no problem. Curious about something? Ask Siri. Or Alexa.

And we still have our old-fashioned libraries and bookstores, too. Think about the many cultures and people who lived before Gutenberg's printing press made mass production of books possible. Can you imagine their reaction if they could step into a Books-A-Million store today? Or their astonishment over a public library where they could borrow any available book of their choice for free?

I have recently indulged in another permissible pleasure: listening to audio books. They keep my mind fascinated when I'm working with my hands. What fun! I guess my inner five year old still likes to have someone read me a story. I'll bet yours does, too.

Michael shared a funny quote with me recently. Question: "If someone from the 1950's suddenly appeared, what would be the most difficult thing to explain to them about life today?" Answer: "I possess a device, in my pocket, that is capable of accessing all the information known to man. I use it to look at pictures of cats and get in arguments with strangers."

~The Pleasure of Simple Joys~

"Sometimes you might feel like no one's there for you, but you know who's always there for you? Laundry. Laundry will always be there for you."

~Facebook meme

It's funny how a single idea can change your life for the better. This happened to me a few years ago when I read the Madame Chic book series, by Jennifer L. Scott. The whole idea is that if we can change our attitudes about the mundane things in life (like laundry), we can change our lives. In these books Jennifer shares what she learned as an exchange student in Paris. As she puts it: "You may think that being chic has nothing to do with the most insignificant and mundane moments of the day. Moments like preparing your meals, emptying your dishwasher, and paying bills. The secret is: those moments aren't insignificant. *Au contraire.* They are very significant. That's right; if you can change your attitude about making the pasta sauce, or choosing your clothes for the day, folding the laundry, setting the table, or dealing with the incoming mail, you can completely change your life." She calls it "becoming a connoisseur" of your own life, by having passion and appreciation for the ordinary. Living with great enthusiasm and curiosity in your everyday life.

French author Robert Arbor gives a great example of this attitude when he says, "...since we're going to eat breakfast anyway, we are going to make it nice." I love it.

These thoughts remind me of a quote I saw on the blackboard at the gym one day: "How you do anything is how you do everything."

And Ecclesiastes 8:15 gives us freedom: "So I commend the enjoyment of life, because nothing is better for man under the sun than to eat and drink and be glad. Then joy will accompany him in his work all the days of the life God has given him under the sun." Amen to that.

So how do we do this? I like to think of ways I can make today an occasion. I am not talking about spending lots of money. Just some simple pleasures. Maybe pulling out that pretty candle someone gave us and lighting it while we are working at our desk or cooking dinner. How about using those good-smelling specialty soaps we have been saving? Maybe we could serve our family dinner on our best china today. I am not really sure why I have been saving mine all these years instead of enjoying it. I recently put one of my fine crystal glasses on my desk as my water glass... because everyone knows that water tastes much better out of fine crystal.

"It's the little things that we do that eventually add up to a happier life. We don't have to change everything about the way we live, but just reconsider some of the details of our daily life. To work more small, everyday pleasures into our days."

In her book, <u>Choosing the Simply Luxurious Life</u>, Shannon Ables suggests "making a mental list of the things that make you smile, lose track of time, or breathe a huge sigh of relief" and then add them into your schedule. Regularly.

~The Pleasure of an Unhurried Pace~

There was a season in my life when I had four small children, and the demands were constant. Some seasons in life are just that way. But I am talking more about our state of mind here, so this could apply even to those busier seasons of life. We have to remind ourselves that *there is enough time* for God to fulfill His purpose in our lives. When we trust Him about this, we will automatically live more in the present. Relax and notice people more. Listen better. We will still work just as hard, and we will still handle problems and opportunities with immediate action, but just without that draining sense of urgency consuming our mental energy and making us feel anxious. And when our minds are relaxed and steady, we will do our best work anyway.

~ The All Important Pleasure of Rich Relationships ~

Enjoying simple pleasures and taking life at an unhurried pace will greatly increase our joy and happiness in life. But the foundation of a well-lived life is having great relationships, because we were made for this. When someone asked Jesus what the most important commands in all of Scripture were, he said:

"'Love the Lord your God with all your heart and with all your soul and with all your mind and with all your strength.' The second is this: 'Love your neighbor as yourself.' There is no commandment greater than these."

(Mark 12:30-31)

That gets me every time. He chose these two commands out of all of Scripture, and said there is no commandment more important than these. It is stunning how much God values relationships! In fact, they are His number one priority, and He wants them to be ours, too. They are the reason and purpose for our lives.

Years ago, I read an inspiring little book called How to Make Someone's Day, by Kathy Peel. It was a list of 365 creative ways to show kindness to others.

Unfortunately, it is out of print now, but I have included thirty-five of her ideas here to get your wheels turning.

1. Drop coins where a child will find them.

2. Serve breakfast in bed to a loved one who's been under stress.

3. Plan a fun outing for someone who's had a hard week.

4. Visit an elderly neighbor.

5. When a friend is due home from a lengthy trip, leave milk, orange juice, and muffins in her refrigerator.

6. Search out a long-lost girlfriend from childhood.

7. Put money in a stranger's expired parking meter.

8. Send flowers for no reason except to say you care.

9. Write a thank you note to your child's teacher.

10. Say thanks with a word or a small gift to someone who faithfully performs a behind-the-scenes job.

11. Ask a mother with small children if you can return her shopping cart for her.

12. Draw a warm bath for a family member who's had a hard day. Fluff and warm his towel in the dryer.

13. When you cook in quantity for your own family, make an extra casserole to give away.

14. Ask if you can pick up a friend's out-of-town relatives at the airport when they arrive for a wedding or funeral.

15. Treat your family like they're company.

16. If you've neglected a friend because of a full calendar, don't remind her of how busy you are. Simply do the best you can to stay in touch, even if it's a short call or text.

17. Schedule a special coffee break for someone at the office. Bring pretty mugs, cinnamon sticks to stir your coffee, and some muffins from home.

18. Ask an elderly person to tell you a story from his or her youth.

19. When someone lives her life in a way that you admire and want to emulate, tell her.

20. Take photos of people and things around you and send them to a friend who's moved away.

21. Ask an elderly neighbor if you can bring her anything from the store when you go.

22. Give someone who looks tired your place in a long line.

23. Over-tip a waitress who looks like she's had a hard day.

24. Don't wait for a special occasion to give someone a present. Out-of-the-blue gifts add joy to any moment.

25. Time spent together cements a relationship. When passing through cities where you have friends, call or write ahead so you can get together, even if it's only for a few minutes.

26. Write "I love you" or "Welcome home" on your driveway or sidewalk to welcome a family member home.

27. Hang red paper hearts in a child's doorway at his or her eye level for a morning greeting.

28. Offer to exercise with a friend who's trying to lose weight.

29. Buy a blank book for a friend who wants to start a journal.

30. Begin a collection for a child. Add to it periodically.

31. Fill an emergency basket for the office with lotion, a small sewing kit, packages of cocoa and chicken broth, cologne, breath mints, pain reliever, and antacids. Invite co-workers to help themselves.

32. When a friend has a new baby, give a present to her older children so they'll feel special.

33. Pack a picnic lunch and take someone special to a surprise location.

34. Have a cookie-baking evening. Make several kinds to take to the office or send to a college student.

35. Pray daily that God will help you see opportunities to be a blessing to others.

~Date Night~

When we had been married about four years, Michael and I made one of the best decisions in our marriage. At the time he was running a new business, and I was at home with our first child, who was two. We decided we'd have a "date night" each week. We didn't know what it would look like, where we'd go, or what we'd do. We just made the decision that we were going to do it, and we wouldn't cancel except for funerals and the stomach bug.

When we first started, we agreed on a few simple things. We would go somewhere quiet and uncrowded, if possible (and it didn't have to be on a Friday or Saturday night, either). On date night, we would not talk about financial things, the kids, or any problems we needed to solve. We would go to places that didn't have big screen TV's. At that time, most people had smaller TV's at home, and big screens were a novelty...and also a complete distraction. Nobody had cell phones at the time either, but when we eventually got phones, we put those up during our date, too. The whole point of date night was to focus on and enjoy each other.

I remember at the time telling my mother-in-law how excited I was, but that the weekly spending for a night out and a babysitter felt a little extravagant for our early-married budget. She wisely told me, "You're not spending. You're investing." It was great advice. From that point on, I never worried about it again. I felt like investing in our marriage was completely worthwhile; something else in the budget could give.

Date night gave us the chance to be "Michael and Margaret" again. Just the two of us, like we were in the beginning. To give our complete attention to each other. And having been through hectic seasons with four small children, and later four teenagers, we have needed that time alone with each other. It has helped us feel like boyfriend and girlfriend instead of "old-marrieds." And three decades later, we still anticipate our date night each week. It is one of our favorite things.

If you got married for the right reasons, chances are that the person you fell in love with and married is deep down still that same person: the person who first caught your eye and attention. When is the last time you focused on those things that intrigued you in the beginning? Consider dating again. If you don't, you are quite possibly missing out on one of the most fabulous permissible pleasures in your life.

~Home, Sweet Home~

Have you ever wondered why God designed us with taste buds, ears, eyes, and a sense of touch? And why He gave us the ability to imagine and create new things? What about the gift of laughter? He has given us such generous gifts. He has given us the ability to create beauty, elegance, and joy in our lives... and what better place to do that than in our homes?

What three words would you use to describe your dream home? If you have trouble thinking of them, think about your favorite place in the world. What is the feeling - the emotion - that place creates in you? How could you recreate those feelings in your own home? And also, how does your favorite place feel to all of your different senses?

~Making Our Homes Beautiful to the Eye~

I want to make our home as beautiful and welcoming as possible, making the most of its assets, and minimizing its weak points. (Pink tub, anyone?) It helps me to pretend I'm a guest or a real estate agent who is seeing our home for the first time. This gives me a fresh perspective. Starting at the front door, what do I notice?

Do I feel welcome? As I pass through each room, what stands out to me, good or bad? What things could I do to make each room more appealing and inviting? As a guest, what would make me fall in love with each of the rooms and make me feel totally at home?

In Creating a Simply SenseSational Home, Terry Willits gives us some great ideas about making our homes beautiful to all of our senses. As Terry says, we are actually creating an atmosphere in our homes. First, I'll share some of her ideas on making our homes visually beautiful. They are simple, but hopefully will stir your creativity and get you thinking of some fresh ways to do things. Since each of us is unique, just use the ideas that appeal to you.

~Have a friendly front door. A pot of flowers. A seasonal wreath or welcome sign. A fresh coat of paint or varnish on your door. Maybe try a brighter shade of paint that pops? Shiny hardware. (You can clean brass with a quality lotion type car wax. Let it dry and then buff.) Clean light fixtures and glass. A polished kick plate. A new welcome mat. Flowers lining the walkway. A flag.

~Transform a room with paint. If you are unsure about a certain color, paint a poster board with it and see how that looks in the daylight and at night. Besides just painting the walls and trim, you could paint the inside of closets or kitchen cabinets, cabinet fronts, an accent wall, wood paneling, furniture, light fixtures, or mirror and picture frames. You could also add a cup of your wall color to white ceiling paint for heightened interest. (The ceiling will slightly reflect the wall color.)

My husband spray painted our mismatching pieces of wicker furniture for our screened porch. Then he dyed the mismatched seat cushions with car vinyl spray dye. (Because vinyl in a car needs to flex, the dye paint has a pliable finish, not a stiff and crunchy one, so it worked beautifully.) Now it looks like all the wicker pieces came as a complete set. And it has held up over time, too. Thanks to my husband, our back porch is one of my absolute favorite rooms in our house.

~Update kitchen cabinets and doors throughout your home with new hardware. Consider replacing cabinet doors with glass front doors. Or simply leave doors off cabinets, paint the interior cabinet walls, and have open shelving.

~Use light to enhance. Light is energizing and inviting. Use three way bulbs to change a room's atmosphere. Place a spotlight on the floor behind a plant or folding screen for indirect light and dramatic shadows. Drape twinkle lights or string them in an indoor tree. (Especially fun in a kid's room.) Hang picture lights to warm the colors of paintings. Install track or recessed lighting to highlight specific areas. Update light fixtures. Enjoy candles grouped together during a meal or when you're taking a bubble bath.

~Create instant impact. Decorate your living room around a focal point, such as a fireplace, special piece of furniture, or a window with a gorgeous view. If possible, have your sofa face the focal point, or have two love seats flank it. A mirror can also create instant impact. It visually expands a room and lightens and brightens a space with its reflection. My husband and I did this in our vanity. The room seemed small and narrow, and a bit dark, too, without a window. So we hung a window-like arched mirror in it, and it transformed the whole look and feel of the room. Another way to add mirrors is to group together many smaller, interesting mirrors on a wall as a collage.

~Create a unique coffee table. Find an old dining room table with character, and cut down the legs. Or create instant "antiques" by brushing or sponging wood stain finish or brown shoe polish onto a plain plaster or concrete sculpture or a hardback book.

~Make your home gorgeous with uncluttered surfaces and fresh flowers. I absolutely love having fresh flowers in our home. I enjoy them in the kitchen and living areas, but also in the bedroom and bathroom. For the bed and bath, I find that a small cobalt blue vase with a few pink roses from our yard is stunning. They feel like the ultimate luxury. It's the high life.

~ What About the Other Senses? ~

~ Sounds, such as music playing softly in the background, can set a great mood in our homes. So can pleasant home sounds like the ticking of a clock. I especially love the songs of the "hot bugs" (cicadas) and crickets on a summer evening when I'm on the back porch. And laughter... it's the best sound of all.

~ Think of how our sense of touch is engaged by the feeling of warmth when a fire is crackling in the fireplace, and we're wrapped in a soft furry blanket while watching a movie on the big screen TV. And then there is the touch of our loved one. Truly, there's no place like home.

~Cookies or bread baking in the oven delight our senses of taste and smell. And who doesn't love coming home to a meal that has simmered all day in the Crockpot, or waking up to the delicious aroma of hot coffee? Speaking of lovely baking aromas, I wanted to share my grandmama's gingerbread and lemon sauce recipe with you. It's such a cozy homemade treat to make in the fall when the leaves are turning orange and red, and it's getting chilly outside.

Katyleene's Gingerbread and Lemon Sauce

Gingerbread Ingredients:

2/3 cup shortening (I have also used unsalted butter.)
1/4 cup sugar
3/4 cup molasses
2 cups sifted all-purpose flour
1 tsp. ginger
3/4 tsp. salt
$1^1/_4$ tsp. baking powder
1/2 tsp. soda
2 eggs, beaten
1/2 cup milk
(Optional: I also add some cinnamon; a little less than 1/2 tsp.)

Gingerbread Directions :

Cream shortening and sugar. Slowly add molasses, beating constantly. Sift together dry ingredients and add 1/2 of them to molasses mixture. Add eggs, and beat well. Add remaining dry ingredients alternately with milk. Pour into a greased and floured 8" cake (or square) pan. Bake in 325 degree oven for about 60 minutes.

Lemon Sauce Ingredients:

1/2 cup butter
1 cup sugar
1/4 cup water
1 egg, well beaten
3 T. lemon juice (about 1 lemon)
Grated rind of lemon (Grate the rind before you cut and
juice the lemon. It's much easier.)

Lemon Sauce directions:

Combine the above ingredients in sauce pan. Cook over
medium heat, stirring constantly, just until mixture comes
to a boil. (Strain sauce if any egg whites show.) Serve
over warm gingerbread.

~Clutter - The Homemaker's Arch Nemesis~

"I tried the Japanese method of decluttering where you hold every object that you own and if it does not bring you joy, you throw it away. So far, I have thrown out all of the vegetables, my bra, the electric bill, the scale, a mirror, and my treadmill."

~ FB meme

This quote really cracked me up. I especially laughed over the bra. But seriously, how do we fight our arch nemesis? Because it really is difficult to have beauty without order.

Most of the time, I think we keep too much stuff because we have a "scarcity mindset." We are afraid we may need the items someday. And another big reason we keep things is guilt or obligation; if someone has given us something, we often feel guilty giving it away, even if we don't really use it. Inherited things can cause us to feel a sense of obligation, too. If we give the items away or sell them, somehow we feel that we are betraying the deceased person, so we feel obligated to keep them.

If you are like me, you have certain areas that are worse than others. It might be good to start decluttering the one that troubles you most. I often remind myself to keep just the things that make my life happier, easier, or are very sentimental to me; but I have to be careful on that sentimental part. That is where I keep way too much stuff. And books, too. I love books.

But I've also found that if I can declutter without making a huge mess, I am much more likely to go ahead and start. Recently, I saw a helpful video about this. The advice was to have a garbage bag for trash and a box for donations, which is typical. But here is the hard part. You deal immediately with an item as soon as you pick it up. Give away, throw away, or go put it up in your house where it actually belongs. (If it doesn't have a place, make a place for it where you think you'd look for it if you needed it.) If you have things that need to be returned to a person or store, then they would go in your car. The thing is, you'll be tempted to make a pile of all the things that go to the car, for example. It may seem inefficient to deal with each item individually and make repeat trips to put things up. But if you use this method, and you get interrupted during your decluttering, you are completely finished up to the point where you stopped. You can really see the progress. And there is nothing to clean up. Besides that, you get lots more steps on your Fitbit.

~An Unexpected Delight~

I'm writing this book during the COVID-19 quarantine. When the quarantine first started, there were so many unknowns. I couldn't help but wonder if there might be shortages of other things besides toilet paper. What if we couldn't get fresh produce for a while? I asked the Lord to take care of us, knowing that He cares. And I also asked him for wisdom to think of some "what?" questions. What positive steps could I take? What was my part?

The answer that came was a delight to me. Let me give you a quick back story first. Last year, my husband and I experienced a lifelong dream. We got to travel to Europe to visit our daughter "Joy", who lives there. She speaks German, and was a fantastic tour guide for us. We saw so many breathtaking things: cathedrals and castles, mountains and lakes in Switzerland, train rides along the Rhine and Mosel rivers, and chocolate. Oh my! But there was a simple thing all over Europe that also charmed me... the beautiful little window boxes full of flowers.

So the answer to my "What?" was to plant a little garden on our balcony. I immediately got to work on it, and it has brought me so much pleasure for six months now.

Thankfully, we haven't had to rely on it, but it is the first thing we see when we open the curtains in the morning. It is both beautiful and practical, and reminds me of our wonderful trip with "Joy." Sometimes it is the little things that make life feel so rich.

~A "Beckoning" Workspace~

My friend Becky gave me great advice when I redid my workspace and desk. She said, "Take everything off your desk and only put back the things you use every single day. Then pick one or two of your very favorite decorative pieces to make your space pretty." She emphasized *very favorite*. And she's right. Now every time I sit down at my desk, I say "ahhhh." It is uncluttered and simply gorgeous to me. It went from a place I didn't enjoy to a place I love. My work has now become a pleasure. Thank you, Becky.

~Exercise~

"Sometimes I want to hide from exercise. Where do I go to sign up for the 'Fitness Protection Program'"?

~Facebook

This quote was funny to me, because I really do feel this way sometimes. Do you? I think most of us sigh and feel guilty when we think about exercise - or the exercise we should be doing. I know that some people genuinely like exercise, but I'm not one of them... and I think I'm in the majority.

Exercise takes lots of energy and exertion; most of us don't enjoy that kind of discomfort. Maybe we don't like for others to watch us in the gym, or we feel self-conscious in our exercise clothes. And we don't like taking the time out of our day to do it. Or we just don't feel up to it. There are many things that make regular exercise something that is hard to be disciplined about. Oh, no! The "D" word. Discipline. It sounds like a dirty word. The kind your mama would wash your mouth out with soap for saying.

Maybe we are telling ourselves all the wrong things. What if we told ourselves that exercise is just "moving our body"? We were made to move. If we could lift the dread of exercise from ourselves and just move more, we would feel better. Moving is good for us and can be fun, too. How about putting on some music and dancing? Taking a walk in the cool early morning or at dusk (alone, or with your best human or furry friend)? Going for a swim if you have access to a pool or lake. Hiking a beautiful trail. You get the idea.

One thing I noticed when we were in Europe was that people got a lot of exercise doing their daily activities. I saw grandmothers riding bikes to the grocery stores. They carried their groceries home in their bike basket or in a backpack. And then, because many apartments there only have stairs, carried them up several flights into their homes. I don't remember seeing many obese Europeans. It is a little harder to grocery shop like that in America, because of the distances between our homes and stores. But we can park a little further from the store door and walk. We can take the stairs when it's possible. Moving is moving, and it all adds up to better health.

Something that helps me with exercise is mentally having a "Plan A" and "Plan B." For example, say my Plan A is to walk in the morning, and I wake up to thunder and pouring down rain. I need to already have my Plan B in mind. Plan B would probably be to do the Stairmaster at home. Actually, I don't have a Stairmaster; I would do the real stairs. And I would have my favorite music playing or listen to a podcast or audio book while I was doing it to make it much more pleasant.

My husband and I do have a gym membership. Michael has lifted weights for years, and has been a great influence on me about that. He once made the comment to me, "I never leave after working out and say 'I wish I hadn't done that.'" This thought keeps me going when I have one of those Fitness Protection Program days.

A thought that can help me keep going in the middle of a difficult exercise is telling myself, "C'mon, just do one. I know you can do one. Great job." And then I tell myself the same thing for the next one. And the next one. It seems silly, but it works. Recently, I heard a marathon runner say something similar. He said he tells himself that all he has to do is get through the next fifteen minutes - and that he can do anything for fifteen minutes. After he gets through that, he focuses on the next fifteen minutes, and that is how he gets through the whole marathon.

I have also noticed that having a workout partner is very helpful. It's just more fun, and when one of you is wavering, the other one is there to say, "C'mon, let's do this thing." You cheer each other on. Two are better than one, Ecclesiastes says. Yes, absolutely.

Lots of times, I think we start exercising to look better or fit our clothes for some special event. Or because our doctor insists. But even if that is the only reason we start, we will soon find out that sleeping better, feeling healthy, having more energy and a quicker mind are extra perks that also come with moving our bodies more. C'mon, let's do this thing!

~Personal Clothing Style~

We have been told "You can't judge a book by its cover," yet many people do. Whether we like it or not, our clothes are an unspoken message to the world, and they often reflect what is on the inside. What we choose to wear daily, or to our child's school, or to an event tells others how we feel about ourselves, and is a reflection on the God we serve. Our clothing affects how we feel, too. We will feel more confident when we make the effort to look our best. And when our style is in line with our personality, we will feel more comfortable in our own skin.

To use an old math term, if there is *congruence* between who we are and our clothing style, our looks will be uniquely magnetic. I can't help but notice that the famous "Proverbs 31 Woman" took time to dress herself well. Prov. 31:22 tells us she wore fine linen and purple. Fine linen in her day was often woven so tightly that it felt a lot like silk. And purple was the color of royalty. I imagine she was very confident, poised, and had quite a presence. She was made in God's image and was a beautiful reflection of Him.

~Creating a Wardrobe We Love~

I did a massive overhaul of my closet about a decade ago. Since I take good care of my clothes, I had lots of clothes that were in good shape, but weren't really suitable anymore. For example, I am embarrassed to admit this, I still had some clothes from college. And I had some beautiful clothes others had given me, but they weren't really my style. So I went through everything, with our then teenaged oldest daughter. She was completely honest with me, often saying things like, "Yes, that fits, but it's not you." or "That looks good, but it doesn't look great." With her help and encouragement, I gave away everything that wasn't the perfect color for me, a flattering fit, *and* totally my style. The short version is that I gave away everything that didn't make me excited to get dressed in the morning.

I gave away over half my closet. Then we went through my accessories and did the same thing. When we finished, I wondered if I would even have anything left to wear. I shouldn't have worried. Afterwards, when I walked into my closet, every single thing in it was something I *loved* to wear. I felt like a kid in a candy shop.

And my closet was so simple, so uncluttered. I could see everything at a glance, and that made it so much easier to come up with creative outfits. And that is what we did. We jotted down outfit ideas in a pretty little notebook, and even noted which undergarments worked best and which accessories made the outfit pop. I could always change things up, but my notebook kept me from having to "reinvent the wheel" if I were in a hurry. We named each outfit to capture the feeling it gave me when I wore it. Here are a few examples straight from the pages of my notebook: Beach Cafe, Soft and Simple, Moonlight in Vermont, Caribbean Breeze, Autumn Joy, Dinner on the Deck, Fire Lit Lodge and Holiday Spirit.

When it comes to fashion and style, it's easy to get confused. But fashion and style are two different things. Fashion is an industry whose survival is based on your feeling that you are missing something in your wardrobe, and that you need the latest trend in order to be beautiful and attractive. In a way, fashion preys on your insecurities. Style, on the other hand, is all about who you are as an individual. It is figuring out what colors look best on you, and what lines flatter your figure. It reveals your personality, too. For example, do you feel most comfortable when you're wearing something that is sporty, classic, dramatic, romantic, or trendy? And style also reflects your lifestyle. What activities do you spend the most time doing?

A really easy way to figure some of these things out is to use your phone to take a picture of your outfit each day for two weeks. It's even better if someone can take the picture for you, because they can more easily get your whole outfit in the picture. Save the pictures in a file on your computer. You will be amazed when you look back at them. You will begin to see your own patterns, both the good ones and the bad ones. Pick out which outfits are your favorites. Why are they your favorites? Try to figure out exactly what it is that you love about them. Is it the color or cut of the clothing? Maybe it is the feel of the material. Why do you feel confident wearing it? This is very useful information. Then notice if there are any outfits that you don't like. What is it about them that you don't like? Be as specific as you can.

If you take the time to consider all these things, you will be able to create a clothing style that is an authentic expression of the real you. You will have that mysterious quality that makes you attractive, distinctive, or special in some way, but is hard to put into words: "that certain something"... or as the French say, "Je ne sais quoi."

~Does Victoria Have a Secret?~

When I walk by the famous lingerie store window, I'm not too sure that Victoria has any secrets. But I do love the idea of beautiful lingerie secretly hidden beneath my clothes. A delicious secret like that really does something for a woman's confidence, as well as her sense of mystery.

I saw a documentary on David O. Selznick and the making of the movie *Gone With the Wind.* All throughout the production of that movie, there were budget issues, and Selznick was criticized for wasteful spending. In particular, he had purchased costly authentic undergarments and skirt hoops for all the women playing Southern belles. These undergarments weren't even going to show in the movie, but Selznick insisted that if the women wore the real thing, they would act like the real thing. He had a point.

Now he had to spend a lot of money on these undergarments for the movie, but today that is not necessary. You can easily find beautiful lingerie for a reasonable price. The main thing is that it fits you well, feels great on your skin, and makes you feel pretty. And there is one more thing... if you buy lingerie that is easy to care for, then it will be simple and effortless to wear something lovely under your clothes everyday.

~A Note on Nighties and Fragrance~

Children have such joy over small pleasures. I smile remembering our kids' excitement each time we bought them new shoes. They often asked if they could sleep in them that first night, and I always said, "Yes!" Now you are probably wondering what this has to do with beautiful nightclothes. Well, the shoes don't have a whole lot to do with nightclothes. But the moral of the shoe story has a whole lot to do with nightclothes. And the moral is to always sleep in something you are excited to wear.

We are all different. You may be enthused about wearing an oversized night shirt, and someone else may love a lacy chemise. To each her own. But just make it something that you look forward to wearing... something that as you slip it over your head at night, gives you a very content feeling, because you look and feel beautiful. Why not?

And what about fragrance? Many style experts suggest having a "signature scent" - one perfume that you wear consistently so that others associate that scent with you.

What a lovely thought. I had a signature scent until "Tatiana" by Diane Von Furstenberg was discontinued. I've never found another one that I love as much as that one, but I am still looking.

In the meantime, I thoroughly enjoy wearing a variety of fragrances. You might catch me sniffing the fragrance on my wrist throughout the day. It is so pleasant. Recently, I found some light colognes by Good Chemistry that are reasonably priced and made with essential oils (no chemicals). I bought a handful of different ones. Now when I get dressed in the morning, I get to pick my "fragrance of the day." I really look forward to it. Fragrance may be invisible, but it is a delightful and powerful permissible pleasure.

~Hairstyle - Your Face's Best Accessory~

Your hairstyle can either hide or accentuate the positive features of your face. Below are some simple tips from Justin Hickox's YouTube channel, and because they are based on art principles, they really do work.

~If you feel that your face looks too long, don't wear styles with too much straight hair along the sides of your face. This lengthens the appearance of your face and make it looked dragged down. Also avoid too much volume on the top. It causes the eye to perceive added length in your face.

~If you feel that your face looks too round, avoid a chin length cut and too much fullness on the sides. Also avoid full bangs, because this "closes out" your face and makes the eye notice width. Instead, increase the fullness of your hair on the top, and it will slim your face.

~If you want to accentuate your eyes, wear your hair in a style that is "open" and off your face, or use a light bang to emphasize and draw attention to your eyes.

~To accentuate cheekbones and lift the eye, create volume in the temple area. Follow the line of your cheekbone (the line that you follow when putting on blush) up into your hair to know where to have volume. The eye will follow this upward line.

~ *Aging With Grace*~

I think we can learn a few things from the French culture on this topic. "Frenchwomen do not aspire to be anyone other than themselves...and they simply aspire to look the best they can *for their age*. They see birthdays as an

85

excuse for a celebration of a life well-lived, full of experience and adventure..." Instead of trying to look twenty-five again, they aspire to be the best version of themselves at whatever age they are. They know that some things like generosity, style, wit, and charm have no expiration date, and that if a woman continues to grow and learn, she develops these qualities more fully over time, as well as developing strength of character. Older women can also possess tremendous wisdom and insight as a result of their varied life trials and adventures. They have learned not to take themselves too seriously. And when a woman has walked with the Lord for many years, she gains a deep trust in His faithfulness that comes from having persevered through many of life's experiences with Him and come out on the other side. She has an indescribable beauty that makes mere physical beauty pale in comparison.

~Where Are the Spoons? How Routines Help~

What if every time you emptied your dishwasher, you put the spoons in a different place in your kitchen? Today, maybe you'd put them in the cabinet above the stove, tomorrow in the pantry...

Every time someone wanted to get a bowl of cereal, they would have to hunt for who knows how long to find a spoon. So much of their time would be wasted each day, searching for something so basic. If they complained to you, your answer might be, "Well, I don't want to have a routine. That hinders my free spirit."

I know it is a silly example, but you can see what I'm saying. We often think of routines as hindering our freedom and "free-spiritedness," when actually they do the opposite. They create more freedom in our lives. Knowing where the spoons are gives a person the freedom to go do the thing she *really* wanted to do. Which is to eat a bowl of cereal. Or ice cream with chocolate fudge sauce, and toasted pecans and whipped cream...in a pink tub...

Routines simplify the things we have to do, so we can get on with the things we want to do. They help us get mundane things done efficiently. In what areas of your life could you use the super power of a good routine? Because it's really nice to have food in the house, gas in the car, and know when our appointments are. When our lives are in chaos, we will be so busy trying to survive that we miss all the good things. When our lives are in order, it's so much easier to notice and enjoy the permissible pleasures God has given us.

~Might These Work for You?~

I have many routines that help me stay organized and productive (such as weekly meal planning), but here are three things that I do that are so simple, they can hardly be called routines. But I do them everyday, because they make my day go much more smoothly. I call them my game-changers. Might they work for you, too?

Here is the first one. Before I go to bed, and while my mind is still "in the game," I pray for wisdom, and write down the five most important things I need to do the next day. If there is something on today's list that I didn't finish, that goes on tomorrow's list. My list is purposely short, and I spend about two minutes jotting it down. Keeping it short forces me to think about what actually needs to be done, and what isn't important. I don't want to waste my life doing unimportant things well! So when I wake up the next morning, I start my day with purpose and direction. There's another small perk of this routine: I think about the next day's dinner, too. So if I need to, I can pull out anything from the freezer and put it in the refrigerator to thaw overnight.

The second one is this. I decide what I will wear the next day by looking at the activities on my list for the next day. I lay my outfit on my bathroom counter or hang it on my closet door, and lay out the lingerie, shoes, and jewelry that go with it, too. This takes about one minute. But it makes my next morning so smooth and easy, and it ties in with my third game-changer.

Working from home has made this third one important. I get in the shower immediately when I get up. I know my clothes are already laid out and waiting for me. If I don't do this, it is way too easy for the day's work to encroach on my self-care, and that doesn't feel good at all. I don't want to look up at lunchtime and realize I'm still in my nighties and haven't even brushed my hair yet. I'd much rather start the day refreshed and put together; it makes for a much more productive day.

~Before New Year's Eve~

The week after Christmas, when everything is in a lull after the big holiday, I like to think and pray about the upcoming year. Before New Year's Eve, I jot those thoughts down. It's nothing too complicated; just two or three goals for each of these areas of my life: my relationship with God, family and friends, finances, health, and hobbies. I try to fit it all on one page if I can. I want to be able to remember everything without having to look at my list all the time. Doing this helps me figure out my priorities and plan some practical ways to live them out. I've been surprised by how much I accomplish when my goals are hands-on and clear... but not necessarily small.

Maybe one spiritual goal would be to read through my Bible in a year; or a financial goal might be to pay a double house note each month (one note being designated towards additional principal). This year, my hobby goal was to take jazz piano lessons. So you can see what I am talking about; the goals are simple, but solid and action-oriented. For example, "Losing weight" is not a goal, but "walking three times a week" or "taking a Zumba class" is. And it is really exciting to see all the results at the end of the year - to see myself growing into the future self I have pictured in my mind.

~Eat That Frog~

"If the first thing you do each morning is to eat a live frog, you can go through the day with the satisfaction of knowing that that is probably the *worst* thing that is going to happen to you all day long."

~Mark Twain

In his book, Eat That Frog, Brian Tracy says your "frog" is your "biggest, most important task, the one you are most likely to procrastinate on if you don't do something about it. It is also the one task that can have the greatest positive impact on your life and results at the moment."

He gives two rules for "eating the frog." He says if you have to eat two of them, eat the ugliest one first. In other words, start with your worst and hardest task first. Start on it and stick with it until it is done before you move on to something else. His second rule is if you have to eat a live frog at all, don't sit and look at it very long beforehand. Just do the worst task first without thinking too much about it.

You may wonder what eating frogs has to do with permissible pleasures. Well, quite a bit. Think of how you feel when a dreaded task is done, and you don't have to think about it anymore. You feel relieved and energized. You don't have something hanging over your head, and it is so much easier to relax. For example, if I were to spend some quality time soaking in my pink tub, but the whole time my mind was filled with anxiety over a task that I needed to do, do you think I would enjoy my bath very much? No, I wouldn't. But what if I am feeling great because I have just finished that dreaded task? I am going to absolutely luxuriate in the tub, my thoughts carefree and easy-going.

Is there any "frog" in your life that is keeping you from fully enjoying every permissible pleasure God has given you? Don't sit and look at it for very long. Just go ahead and eat that frog.

~The Bigger Pleasures~

"Not only did I fall off the diet wagon, I dragged it into the woods, set it on fire, and used the insurance money to buy Twinkies."

~ Facebook meme~

We are going to have conflicting thoughts and feelings sometimes. Especially about food. And it is true that we get to choose which feeling we act on. But it's not that simple. Humans tend to move towards pleasure and away from pain, so when it comes to Twinkies, it is easy to gravitate towards the pleasure rather than denying ourselves. With regards to dieting, it is not likely that we are going to be able to sustain a lifestyle that feels like pain and denial everyday. So maybe broadening what we view as pleasure can really help us. Like feeling good about our body or happy with how our clothes fit; loving the way it feels to have a soft dress slipping over a healthy body. These are pleasures, too. Actually, they are the much bigger pleasures. And if I had to pick between pleasures, I would pick the bigger ones.

~An Eating Plan for Life~

The only way we are going to be successful in keeping a healthy weight is having an eating plan that works for life. All of our life. That is a tall order, no?

About twenty years ago, I discovered I was gluten intolerant. This was before there were hundreds of gluten-free options in the stores; at the time there were none. I faced a radical change in my diet if I wanted to feel good again.

Overnight, I had to quit eating all pasta dishes, bread, pizza, sandwiches and hamburgers. No fried foods, burritos or quesadillas, or any casseroles made with cream soup. And the dagger in my heart... no cake, pie, doughnuts, or cookies. It was a huge change; especially for a Southern girl raised on fried chicken and biscuits.

But this experience has taught me a very valuable lesson. I learned to focus on all the good things that I could have; the delicious foods that increased my health and energy. This helped me mentally adjust to uprooting my entire way of cooking and eating. Otherwise, I would have always been pining away for all the "forbidden fruit" I could no longer have. I knew one thing. I did *not* want to spend the rest of my life feeling like I was deprived and missing out, because self-pity is self-destructive.

So I made a list of everything I could eat. Any meat or seafood seasoned with salt, pepper, and herbs. Rice, corn, and a few other grains. All the fruits, veggies, eggs, and nuts that I wanted. When I focused on the choices that I did have, I didn't feel so deprived anymore.

And that is how it is with any eating plan. Our weight management will be more successful if we focus on the positive choices we do have - the foods that bring us radiant health *and* pleasure. Because pleasure when we eat is totally important, too. Have you considered making a list of all the high-quality foods that you love to eat, or that you would like to eat more often? Because focusing on pleasure and quality helps us reduce our focus on quantity.

Thankfully, I generally don't have a weight problem. But having had four children, I know how it feels to have those twenty extra pounds to lose. A couple of habits have helped me in staying slim. Of course, "life happens," but I try not to eat standing up or in the car if possible. If I eat "on the run" like that, I am tempted to eat lower quality food, and too much of it. And I don't savor my food as much. But if I take the time to sit down and eat, I usually pick "real" food and eat a healthier, more nutritious meal.

My second habit is not snacking between meals. Snacking tends to put unwanted pounds on me. I have a hearty appetite, so I'd rather eat satisfying portions of food at a meal than to graze all day. Then after the meal, I go ahead and brush my teeth and don't eat again until the next meal.

Maybe one of the reasons snacking adds pounds is what I would eat if I did snack. Probably not fruit or veggies. I'm not a celery stick kind of gal... more like chocolate covered almonds, or chips and dip. Also, snacking is usually a little too open-ended. What exactly is the portion size if the food is not on a plate where I can see it? I probably don't want to know.

The great thing about not snacking is that we'll be genuinely hungry when we do sit down to eat, and very excited about our meals. It is incredibly pleasurable. I have heard that the difference between a good meal and a great one is one hour. (Note: Do not apply this rule when showing hospitality.) One more thing... it is not smart to wait too long between meals. It's easy to eat anything we can find if we get past the point of no return. (Maybe you wouldn't, but I would.)

But here is the happy news of the day. When we focus on pleasure and eating high quality foods, *no food* ever has to be off limits as a special treat... as a permissible pleasure. Can you feel the freedom? We just need to R-E-S-P-E-C-T ourselves and make sure that it is a special treat, not an everyday habit.

~A Little Caramel Cake~

Years ago (before my gluten problem), my dad came to visit us, and he brought us a homemade caramel cake that my sister Katy had made. Katy is an excellent cook, and the cake was luscious. We set it on the end of the counter in the kitchen, and after a few days, most of the cake was gone. I told my dad, "Please tell Katy how much we've all enjoyed her cake." He said, "Margaret, I haven't had any." I'm sheepish to tell you this, but I eventually realized that "we all" hadn't enjoyed that cake. I had. I had nibbled over several days, and had eaten most of that cake all by myself. Now because my dad was a general practitioner, I took his next comment seriously. He told me, "Well, that's OK. Sometimes you just need a little caramel cake for your health." Thank you for the wise medical advice, Daddy.

~SF Agent~

My neighbors and I have a running group text. It's funny, and it has been especially enjoyable during this Covid quarantine. The other day, one neighbor texted that she'd talked with her SF Agent about an event that had been cancelled due to Covid. Another neighbor asked what an SF Agent was. The first neighbor explained that it was her State Farm agent. "Oh," said the second neighbor, "I thought SF Agent meant 'Special Functions Agent'"! Made me smile. I really liked that, because that is what we are every time we invite someone into our homes. Hospitality is all about being a Special Functions Agent.

Covid has put a damper on having friends over lately, but one thing we have done in the past that's been a lot of fun in our neighborhood is to have a "Dessert Night." Each neighbor brings a different dessert and everybody gets to sample of all the goodies on the "dessert buffet." Whoever hosts simply supplies paper plates and napkins, forks, and an ice chest full of drinks. Very easy and fun, and there's lots of laughter.

My friend Karen is a mentor to many younger women. Her wisdom on hospitality is to find one meal that you make especially well, and serve that meal each time you have guests. Make it your specialty. Over time, of course, you will find other meals that work well too, but if you have one signature meal, then having people over will feel very comfortable and natural to you. You will be able to focus on your guests instead of meal preparation, which is the whole point.

Karen's signature meal is **Pork Slider Sandwiches**, a veggie tray with dip, a fruit tray, and a dessert. But the pork sandwiches have a little special twist. I will share what she did, because it was simple, yet so delicious. She seasoned a pork tenderloin with a mixture of half Dale's Sauce and half Italian dressing, then grilled it and sliced it. She also caramelized onions, by slicing and cooking them in a skillet over low heat in a small amount of oil, stirring when needed. She cooked them for at least 30 minutes or until soft and brown. (Allow one whole onion for each person.) And she made a whipped feta spread, too.

Karen's Whipped Feta

Ingredients:

8 oz. feta cheese, crumbled and at room temperature
3 oz. whipped cream cheese, at room temperature

Directions:

Add crumbled feta to a food processor and pulse until small crumbs remain. Add in cream cheese and puree for 4-5 minutes, scraping down the sides when necessary, until feta is super creamy.

To serve the pork sliders, spread two slices of a baguette with the feta spread. Pile the meat and onions on one slice. Top with the other slice. The combination of different flavors is really delectable!

~ When Things Don't go as Planned ~

As a hostess (SF Agent), sometimes even our best plans may not work out quite like we thought. Laura Calder, in The Inviting Life, advises us not to apologize for our food, no matter how badly we want to. She says if we really mess something up, it's much better to make a joke about it, then don't mention it again. For example, "My 'chocolate mystery' here, tastes especially good when you hide it under a lot of whipped cream and can't actually see it."

It is OK to mess up. Often, others will feel more comfortable having us over to their homes when we've made an honest mistake like that. They know that if they mess something up when we are at their house, we'll understand.

~ Some Musings on Cooking ~

We live in a wonderful time; when it comes to cooking, we don't have to do the hard part any more. I have heard stories of my great grandmother that make me very grateful for this. Let me explain. When I want a roast chicken dinner, I pick up a chicken at the store; I get to choose whether I want rosemary and lemon to fill the cavity, or maybe some apples, celery, and onions. I get to decide what to season the skin with, and then I pop it into my oven and await deliciousness. My great grandmother, on the other hand, had to catch the chicken. Then she had to swing it around and around her head to wring its neck. Next, she had to pluck out all of the feathers, and quite often, they did not want to come out. It was bloody, messy work. Eventually, she would get to the cooking part. There was so much work involved in just obtaining the food. I feel highly privileged because I get to do the creative part in the kitchen without all of that hard work.

At the end of a work day when I'm feeling tired, but need to start cooking, I have to remind myself about these things. I turn on some upbeat music, light a candle on my counter, and grab a cold or hot drink to sip as I cook. Rachel Ray has often said that cooking is therapy. The aromas of food cooking, the sizzling of garlic in olive oil, the tastes, and the bright colors. The rhythm of chopping and dicing. It's good for the soul. She is absolutely right.

~Out of the Mouth of Babes~

One day when our kids were little, I decided to take each of them individually to Dairy Queen to get a treat.

I particularly remember buckling our three year old "Joy" into her booster seat beside me in our 1972 Pontiac Catalina (my husband likes old cars). I told her I was going to get a chocolate milkshake. I asked her what she was going to get. She adorably answered, "A chocolate ("chock-it") shake. 'Cause I'm a woman, and you're a woman, and womans likes chocolate!" Oh my. The wind wasn't blowing at all when that apple fell from the tree. Bless her heart.

I admit I am a chocoholic. But the upside to that is that I'm going to share a fabulous chocolate dessert recipe with you. I have yet to meet someone who doesn't like this dessert. The recipe uses ingredients you usually have on hand, too, so you can bake one up quickly if you have a dessert emergency. And it is almost scandalous if you serve it warm with a scoop of vanilla ice cream. So without further ado, here is my sister-in-law Twila's Fudge Pecan Pie recipe. Because sometimes you need a little fudge pecan pie for your health.

Twila's Fudge Pecan Pie

Ingredients:

1 cup sugar
1/8 teaspoon salt
$3^1/_2$ TBSP cocoa
1 (5 oz.) can evaporated milk (NOT sweetened condensed milk)
2 eggs
1 TBSP vanilla (yes, a tablespoon)
1/2 stick butter, melted
1/2 cup chopped pecans
1 frozen unbaked pie shell (I like Marie Callender's)

Directions:

Whisk together dry ingredients in a bowl. Add remaining ingredients. Mix thoroughly. Pour into unbaked pie shell. Bake at 350 degrees for 30 minutes or until set.

~What are You Waiting For?~

My father-in-law was eighty when he saw a car online that he liked. Since he was not especially eBay literate, and my husband is, he asked Michael to check it out for him. Michael looked into it and found the car not only to be a good deal, but also to be just what my father-in-law had been considering for quite some time. When he reported back to his dad, his dad replied, "Well, I think I'll wait." I remember Michael saying to him, "You're eighty years old. What exactly are you waiting for?" That conversation has stayed with us; sometimes we ask ourselves the same thing. I wonder why we instinctively defer to hesitating and waiting. What are we waiting for? Now, please don't use this book as a justification to go and buy the car you want. That is not what I'm saying.

What I am saying is there are so many positive things that we could start to do right now, at this very moment in our lives, but we hesitate. Why do we do that? And there are many permissible pleasures right in front of us today that we have not even noticed or enjoyed. What exactly are we waiting for?

~Coming Full Circle ~

I hope that reading this book has inspired or motivated you in some way, big or small. We all benefit from having a healthy mindset. It is a gift in itself. It is also the foundation for taking the outward actions that will greatly enhance the quality of our lives. My prayer is that a healthy mindset and intentional actions will become a part of who we are every day.

We each have some gifts sitting unopened right in front of us. What does that say to the Giver? It is time for us to go ahead and rip that wrapping paper off. Time to open and use those gifts. Especially His gracious gift of choice. We get to choose whether we will guard our hearts or not. We choose how we talk to ourselves, and whether we accept and like ourselves as He made us. It is time for us to choose whether we live our lives trying to please and impress others (What will "they" think?) or to please God. And to choose whether to compare ourselves to others or just compare ourselves to ourselves.

We also get to choose whether we accept the things we can't change and deliberately change the things that we can. And whether or not we live our lives filled with gratitude and contentment. We get to decide how we frame problems in our minds; whether we ask "why?" or "what?" during difficult situations. And He gives us freedom to choose how we think about our past, too. Do we dwell on it, feeling broken and ashamed, and letting it define us because we can't accept His forgiveness? Or do we learn from it, knowing that He will redeem our past, and that we are a good work in progress? And we get to choose how we use our imaginations about the future, too. Do we imagine doom and gloom, or do we use this fantastic gift to imagine what our lives could become?

Not only does He give us the tremendous gift of freedom of choice, but He also gives us many other permissible pleasures - simple joys - in our daily lives. So now is the time to get in our pink tub. Light that candle we have been "saving." Eat our Cheerios out of our fine china bowl. And thank God the whole time we are doing it. It is time to recognize the tremendous love that motivates all of His gifts to us, tangible and intangible, and not to take his love and blessings for granted. He designed us to enjoy and appreciate all these pleasures He gives us, and He wants us to taste and see that He is good.

And the most lavish gift of all is that He designed us to have a relationship - a friendship - with Him. To live our lives full of joy in the Giver Himself as we experience His love and love Him back.

Epilogue

Having a relationship with God is a gift beyond words. It is far greater than a mere "permissible pleasure." In fact, it is the source of all "permissible pleasures" and is definitely something we don't want to forfeit. Unfortunately, there is something that gets in the way of our having a relationship with Him - our sins. The good thing is, Jesus comes to us in our "before" mode. It doesn't matter how much of a hot mess we are or have been in the past. He will forgive everything we have ever done if we will confess it to Him and ask Him to forgive us. He can already see the unique person we will become as He transforms us into all we were created to be.

I like the way Michael Ramsden explains it. "Sometimes we struggle with the idea that there is a Design and a Designer. The message of the Gospel is that you and I were created; we were designed. We were brought into existence by a loving God. That is where it starts - with some wonderful good news. And what is more, we were created in the image of God. We reflect Him.

However, instead of accepting God and accepting how we should live, we decided we could do a better job living our way. We rebelled against Him. We were created one way, but something seems to have gone wrong within our very being, the inside of us. Now things aren't the way they should be.

We look at the suffering in the world, and think, 'It shouldn't be this way!' Same for the struggles in our own hearts and lives. We were created in the image of something beautiful, and we've fallen away from it.

So if there's to be any hope and joy in this world, we need someone to come and change who we are. To change the nature of our existence. To enable us to become *that which we were always intended to be*. And this is what the Christian good news is all about.

God comes into this world as Jesus Christ. And when He goes onto the cross, He takes into his being, into his person, everything that's gone wrong in yours and mine. All the wrong thoughts you and I've ever had, all the bad things we've done, and all the harmful things that have been done to us. He takes on all of that. Through his death and his resurrection, He pays the terrible consequences for the things that have robbed us of who we should be. And He comes to every single human being, every human heart, and he offers us a new birth, a new life, a new start in Him."

He wants to give us this new life. It starts when we ask Him to forgive our sins and the wrong things we have thought and done in our lives. We can tell Him anything, because His love and his mercy for us will never change. If we don't feel close to him right now, we can tell Him that, too. We can ask Jesus to draw us closer. We matter so much to Him. It is the one thing in life that we can count on. Forever.

Notes

Accepting Ourselves:

The story about the woman starting to date again: Guy Winch; "Why We all Need to Practice Emotional First Aid"; TEDx Linnaeus University; November 2014.

Not a Hot Mess Any More:

The quote "Life begins at the end of our comfort zone": Little Book of Life: A User's Manual, by Neale Donald Walsh.

Charles Stanley quote, "Anything that God does in your life will last....": God's Way perpetual calendar, May 7 devotion, by Charles Stanley.

"I Wish I...":

The concept of walking 20 minutes a day making you leaner and more fit without changing anything in your diet: Thirty Chic Days, Fiona Ferris, 2016, p.174.

The quote: "Don't discount any action as being 'too small'...": Thirty Chic Days, Fiona Ferris, 2016, p.174.

Don't Ask "Why?"; Ask "What?":

Tim Keller quote, "God will either give us what we ask for in prayer, or He will give us what we would've asked for if we knew everything He knows.": Lou Giglio video on Intimacy with God; Ravi Zacharias International Ministry; April 27, 2020.

Tomorrow is Your Future:

The brain's "negativity bias": "Our Brain's Negative Bias: Why our Brains are More Highly Attuned to Negative News"; Psychology Today; Hara Estroff Marano; June 20, 2003.

"The me of five years from now": Lena Kay; "Three Steps to Transform Your Life"; TEDx Nishtiman; May 15, 2017.

Our mental picture of ourselves has a powerful effect on our behavior: Eat That Frog; Brian Tracy, Berrett-Kohler Publishers; 2017, p. 6.

Our Mark on the World:

"Do we ever really know which mark we make matters the most?": The Broken Way, by Ann Voskamp, Zondervan, 2016.

Play First; Work Second:

"Play first; work second. It stimulates our passion.": Dr. Shimi Kang; TEDx Kelowna; September 28, 2014.

The Pleasure of Simple Joys:

"You may think that being chic has nothing to do with the most insignificant and mundane moments of the day. Moments like preparing your meals, emptying your dishwasher...": At Home with Madame Chic; Jennifer L. Scott, Simon and Schuster; 2014, p.4.

"...since we're going to eat breakfast anyway, we are going to make it nice": Joie de Vivre; Robert Arbor; Simon and Schuster; 2003, p. 2.

"It's the little things that we do that eventually add up to a happier life. We don't have to change everything about the way we live, but just reconsider some of the details of our daily life. To work more small, everyday pleasures into our days.": Joie de Vivre; Robert Arbor; Simon and Schuster; 2003, p. 194.

"...making a mental list of the things that make you smile, lose track of time, or breathe a huge sigh of relief": Choosing the Simply Luxurious Life; Shannon Ables; Simply Luxurious Publishing; 2014, p. 15.

Making Our Homes Beautiful to the Eye:

Terry Willits' ideas on making our homes beautiful: 505 Quick Tips to Make Your Home SenseSational; Terry Willits; Zondervan Publishing House; 1996.

Clutter - The Homemaker's Arch Nemesis:

Ideas for decluttering: "How to Declutter WITHOUT Making a Mess"; The Minimalist Mom (YouTube video based on the book Decluttering at the Speed of Life, by Dana White); July 8, 2020.

Hairstyle - Your Face's Best Accessory:

Hairstyle tips to accentuate the positive features of your face: "Hair Mistakes That Age You Faster"; Justin Hickox; YouTube, July 7, 2020.

A Quick Note on Aging with Grace:

"Frenchwomen do not aspire to be anyone other than themselves...and they simply aspire to look the best they can *for their age*. They see birthdays as an excuse for a celebration of a life well-lived, full of experience and adventure...": Forever Chic; Tish Jett, Rizzoli ex libris; 2013, p.14.

"They know that some things like generosity, style, wit, and charm have no expiration date.": Forever Chic; Tish Jett, Rizzoli ex libris; 2013, p.16.

Eat That Frog:

Brian Tracy quote: Your "frog" is your "biggest, most important task, the one you are most likely to procrastinate on if you don't do something about it. It is also the one task that can have the greatest positive impact on your life and results at the moment.": Eat That Frog; Brian Tracy, Berrett-Kohler Publishers; 2017, p.2.

The Bigger Pleasures:

The concept of broadening what we view as pleasure, like feeling good about our body or happy with how our clothes fit: 30 More Chic Days; Fiona Ferris; 2018, p. 259.

When Things Don't go as Planned:

"My 'chocolate mystery' here, tastes especially good when you hide it under a lot of whipped cream and can't actually see it.": The Inviting Life; Laura Calder; Appetite by Random House; 2017, p. 155.

Epilogue:

Michael Ramsden's explanation of the Gospel: "The Saturday Session" produced by RZIM (Ravi Zacharias International Ministries); May 10, 2020.

Acknowledgements

(Because my mama always told me: "Don't forget to say thank you.")

Jesus - Thank you for saving me and loving me. I want to please you above all else.

Michael - My outstanding husband and my best friend. I've never met another man like you. I appreciate your steady love, support, and strength. Thank you for being my editor-in-chief. And for the best permissible pleasures in my life.

Jeremy - You're the one who originally told me the Permissible Pleasures quote. And thank you for patiently repeating it to me until I had it in my head, and could get home from the gym to write it down!

Yvette - My faithful prayer partner for many years. For so long, the Lord has met with us, guided us, and answered our prayers. My life would have been very different without your loyal friendship and your wisdom. God gave me an irreplaceable gift in you.

Betty - You've been a dear friend to me since college. You've always seen the good in me and lovingly let me know that. And you've taught me so much about serving others. I'm immensely grateful for your godly example and prayers.

Amy Soloman - My childhood playmate, you strongly encouraged me to write a book when you were texting me after my Mama's death. Thank you, my sweet friend. Don't ever underestimate the power of your encouraging words to motivate others.

My three sisters: Katy, Elizabeth, and Jo - Since both Mama and Daddy have passed on, it's just the four of us now. I can see so much of Mama and Daddy in each of you. And I love you very much.

Kristie Baker - Your delightful friendship and upcoming visit inspired me to actually start writing this book; to surprise you with a gift to refresh you while you're here, because you always like to learn and grow. You're very contagious in the good way! I hope you like it.

118

A Note from the Author

Thank you for reading this book. I hope these ideas will make a difference for you like they have for me, and that ultimately they will make your life more abundant. This hope compelled me to write in the first place and kept me going on the days when I wanted to quit.

I'd love to hear what was most helpful to you... which ideas you have put into action, and what results you have experienced. And if you have any questions, I'd be glad to try to answer those, too.

You may contact me at: margaretdarnell00@gmail.com or www.permissiblepleasures.com.

Many blessings,
Margaret

120

About the Author

Margaret Darnell hails from the Deep South, and is a devoted wife and mother. After homeschooling for many years, she now works with her husband in their wireless technology company. She loves playing the piano, any outside activities that involve water, old car shows, and being in the kitchen. She is particularly grateful for the permissible pleasures of chocolate, coffee, a good book, and fresh flowers.

Made in the USA
Columbia, SC
10 August 2021